The contest

It is summer in Scotland.

The sun is hot.

All the fuzzbuzzes are out in the glen.

They are not going on a haggis hunt.

They are getting ready for a contest.

All of them can go in for this contest.

Some of them will win a medal.

Next to the crofts there is a big red and blue tent.

A tent as big as this is called a big top.

At the end of the contest they will all go into this tent.

They will eat a big dinner.

Draw the tent and colour it in.

Write

In summer the fuzzbuzzes have a contest.

Some of them will win a medal.

A

Black Angus is still grumpy.

This is because he cannot win a medal.

Every summer he tells himself that he is going to win a medal.

Every summer he ends up without one.

This summer he is going to have just one more go.

This is his last contest.

Write

Black Angus cannot win a medal.

This is why he is so grumpy.

M
M

This is the first contest.
It is called the slippery log.
Can you see it?
The slippery log is a big tree trunk.
There is wet brown mud on top of it.
It is very very slippery.
There is some more thick wet mud on the grass under the log.
The fuzzbuzzes have to go across the log without coming off.
The first one to get across will win the first medal.
Macfuzz the buzz is next to the log.
He will get things going.
Can you see a gun in his hand?

Draw the slippery log.

Write

The first contest is the slippery log.

Windbag goes first.

Splash!

He sits down in the wet brown mud.

He picks himself up but he is not very happy.

There is thick wet mud on his orange and yellow kilt.

He has to mop it off.

Jock goes next.

How will he do?

Splash!

He ends up in the wet mud as well.

Little Don goes next.

How will he get on?

Splash!

Now the thick mud is on his bonnet.

Angus is ready for his go now.
The chief gives him a hand up.
The log is still very slippery
but Angus has his stick to help him.
How will he get on?
Splash!
Black Angus does not do very well.
Down into the thick mud he goes!
Angus is very upset.
He goes off to his croft
to mop himself up.

Write

Angus cannot get across the log.

Draw him as he drops off.

In the end Tosh gets up.

He is the last one to go.

But he has his umbrella to help him.

He puts on his two big boots as well.

His boots stick to the mud on the log.

Tosh does not trip up.

He runs from end to end without a stop.

Tosh is very happy.

Macfuzz asks him to get up onto a box.

Now Macfuzz can pin his medal on.

Draw Tosh going across the log.

Write

Tosh runs across the slippery log.

He gets the first medal.

The clan get ready for the next contest.

This is called kick the pom-pom.

In this contest they have to kick a pom-pom into a big net.

Big Ben has to stop the pom-pom from going in.

The first one to go is Tosh.

He runs up to the pom-pom.

He is going to have a very big kick.

But one of his boots comes off.

Where does it go?

Can you see it?

The chief is mad.

He tells Tosh off.

Write

The next contest is called kick the pom-pom.

A

The next one to go is Black Angus.
He puts the pom-pom down on the grass.
Next he runs back to the end of the glen.
The clan can just see him.
Now he runs up as fast as he can.
He runs up to the pom-pom.
Crack! He hits it.
What a big kick!
The pom-pom goes very fast.
Crack!
It goes crashing into the crossbar.
But it does not go into the net.
Black Angus is fed up.

Write

Black Angus is fed up.
His pom-pom hits the crossbar.

Hilda comes out next.

The clan love her big yellow boots.

She runs up to the pom-pom
and she gives it a very big kick.

The pom-pom goes as fast as a jet.

All the fuzzbuzzes duck.

The pom-pom hits Black Angus.

Crack!

Now it goes across to the net.

It is still going very fast.

Ben jumps up to get it.

It is a very good jump but
he cannot stop the pom-pom.

It drops under the crossbar and
into the back of the net.

How astonishing!

Hilda is going to win a medal.

M
The jumping contest

The chief pulls out the last medal.

Can you see it?

It is yellow with a blue and green ribbon.

There are some words on the medal.

Can you read them?

The chief tells the clan that the last contest is called jumping the river.

The first one to jump across the river will win the last medal.

Angus will not go in for this contest.

He does not jump very well at all.

He goes across to the river bank.

He is very very upset.

He will not win a medal now.

Write

Angus cannot win a medal now.

The first one to have a go at jumping across the river Mac is Big Ben.

But a little rock trips him up.

Splash!

What a shock!

He goes into the river.

His kilt is wet.

His vest is wet.

There is a frog on top of his bonnet.

It has come down from a pond in the hills.

The frog jumps back into the river.

Draw Ben in the river Mac.

Write

Big Ben ends up in the river.

He is very wet.

Don is getting hot.
He has to fan himself with his bonnet.
He jumps next.
Splash!
He ends up in the river.
He is not so hot now.
The next one to have a go is Tosh.
Splash!
He ends up in the river as well.
He is all wet and his boots are full up.
Can you see the little green frog?
Now Jock has a go.
He pulls back the zip on his pocket.
He is getting something out.
It is a big spring to help him.
How will he get on?
Splash!
His spring is not very good.

The little fuzzbuzzes are in a ring.

They are up to something.

They are going to play a trick on Black Angus.

Can you see a fuzzbuzz with a blue cap?

There is a big pin in his hand.

What is he going to do with it?

Black Angus is still next to the river.

He is very very grumpy.

The little fuzzbuzz creeps up on him.

In goes the pin and up goes Angus.

What a shock!

He goes up and up and up.

A

Down comes Black Angus.

He comes crashing down, just missing a big rock.

He drops into some trees.

Can you see him?

But he is not on this bank of the river.

Black Angus is across the river!

It is astonishing.

He is going to win the last medal.

Write

Black Angus jumps across the river.

He will get a medal at last.

The jumping contest

The clan go into the big red and blue tent.

Macfuzz gives Angus his medal.

Hilda gives him a big cup.

Windbag gets out his bagpipes and Jock gets ready to sing.

Don is ready to eat some haggis.

All the clan are there.

Angus is very very happy.

He has a medal at last!

Where will the clan go for dinner?

What colour is the tent?

What is the tent called?

Why is Black Angus so grumpy?

What is the first contest called?

What contest does Hilda win?

Why does Macfuzz get mad at Tosh?

Where does the little frog end up?

What does Jock get out of his pocket?

Write out these words and write in the missing letters.

c _ ntest m _ dal _ pset

h _ ggis W _ ndbag